Dr. Seuss Workbook
PRESCHOOL

Contents

READING

EXPLORE YOUR WORLD!

Throughout this book, you'll find activity pages that encourage kids to learn and explore everywhere. These pages don't follow the specific learning goals of the lessons. They are meant to expand learning beyond the book, sending kids searching, counting, and crafting all around the house—and even outside!

MATH

FEELINGS

SCIENCE

Dear Parents,

There's a world of learning inside the pages of this workbook, and your child will get the most out of it with your support. Here are some tips:

- Encourage your child. Positivity is important, especially when your child finds a task frustrating or difficult!

- Make sure your child has a quiet, comfortable place to work.

- Read the activity directions with your child.

- Give your child a variety of colored pencils and markers to write down the answers and draw pictures.

- Check your child's answers and gently guide your child to the correct response if it wasn't his or her first choice.

- Spend extra time with your child on the areas that he or she finds difficult.

- Pull out your child's best work and display the pages around your home.

READING →

The more that you **READ**, the more things you'll **KNOW**. The more that you **LEARN**, the more places you'll **GO**.

Collect your stickers at the end of each lesson.

A, B, C, and D

There's so much to do, there's so much to see, all with the letters A, B, C, and D!

Color each letter.

A B

C D

Color the letters A, B, C, and D.

APPLE

BALL

CAKE

DOG

The Letter A

BIG

A

little

a

apple

Trace, then write big letter A.

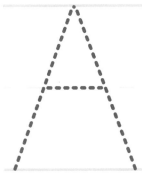

Trace, then write little letter a.

Circle every A and a.

The Letter B

BIG   little

B b

book

Trace, then write big letter **B**.

Trace, then write little letter **b**.

Draw paths to every B and b.

B e c o B b

The Letter C

BIG **C** little **C**

cat

Trace, then write big letter C.

Trace, then write little letter c.

Connect each car to a C or c.

The Letter D

BIG   little

D d

dog

Trace, then write big letter D.

Trace, then write little letter d.

14

Circle every D and d.

c d

e s

D Z

R N

j k

d x

A, B, C, and D

E, F, G, and H

More wonderful letters are waiting for you. Meet E, F, G... and the letter H, too!

Color each letter.

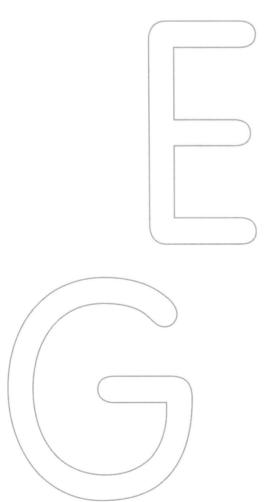

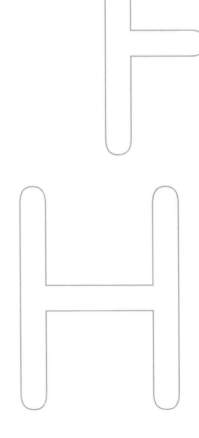

Color the letters E, F, G, and H.

 EGG

 FISH

 GOAT

 HAT

The Letter E

BIG

E _{little} e

elephant

Trace, then write big letter **E**.

Trace, then write little letter **e**.

Color every egg that has an **E** or **e**.

The Letter F

BIG   little

F f

fox

Trace, then write big letter **F**.

Trace, then write little letter **f**.

Circle every **F** and **f**.

The Letter G

BIG
little

G g

giraffe

Trace, then write big letter **G**.

Trace, then write little letter **g**.

Connect each goat to a G or g.

p

g

k

G

o

j

g

m

a

e

G

H

The Letter H

BIG   little

H h

hippopotamus

Trace, then write big letter H.

Trace, then write little letter h.

Draw paths to every H and h.

E, F, G, and H

YOU DID IT!

Forest Forever!

How many pink trees do you see?
How many yellow trees do you see?

Now let's explore the real trees in your world. Look outside or, better yet, go for a walk with an adult. Try to spot the tallest tree as far as you can see.

ONCE-LER WAGON

I, J, K, and L

You'll be ready to read and spell, once you've learned **I, J, K** and **L!**

Color each letter.

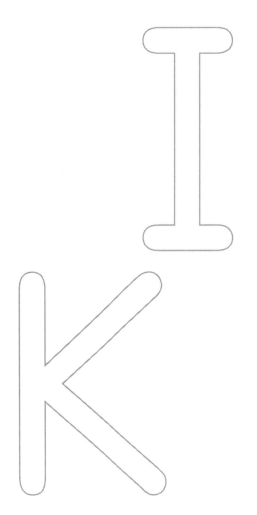

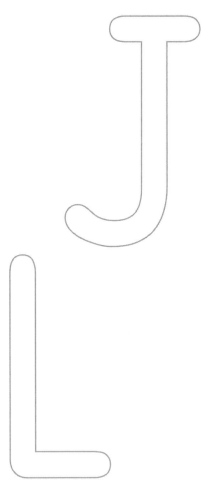

Color the letters I, J, K, and L.

 INK

 JAM

 KITE

 LEMON

The Letter I

BIG   little

I i

itch

Trace, then write big letter I.

Trace, then write little letter i.

Circle every I and i.

k

i

r

O

A

i

W

Y

i

b

I

j

p

The Letter J

BIG   little

J j

jam

Trace, then write big letter **J**.

J

Trace, then write little letter **j**.

j

Color every jar that has a **J** or j.

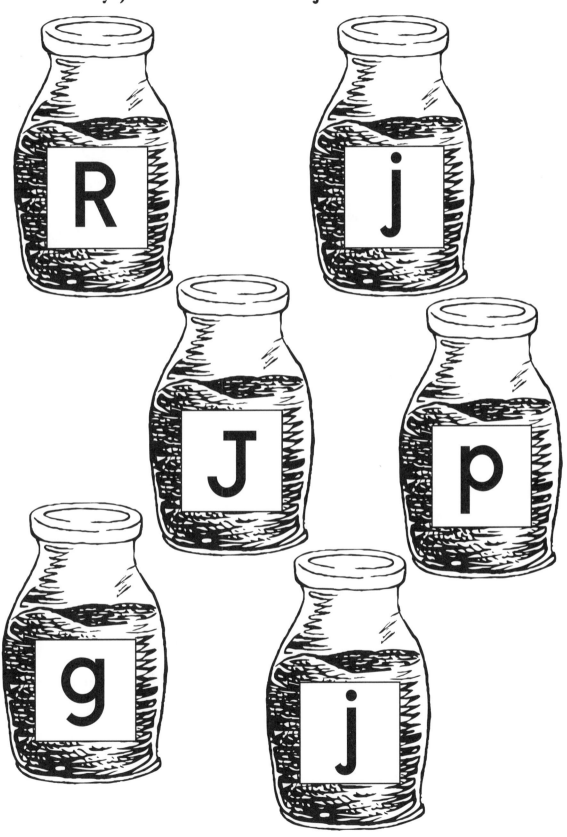

The Letter K

BIG   little

K k

kangaroo

Trace, then write big letter K.

Trace, then write little letter k.

Circle every K and k.

The Letter L

BIG   little

L l

lion

Trace, then write big letter L.

Trace, then write little letter l.

Connect each lime to an L or l.

P

L

r

y

l

l

j

d

J

L

U

I, J, K, and L

YOU DID IT!

M, N, O, and P

More letters are waiting for you and me. Here are the letters M, N, O, and P!

Color each letter.

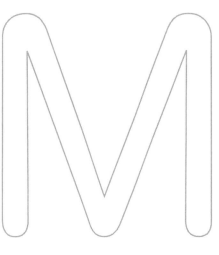

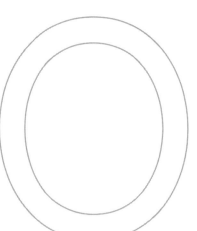

Color the letters M, N, O, and P.

MOUSE

NET

OWL

PAN

The Letter M

BIG

Mm

little

monkey

Trace, then write big letter **M**.

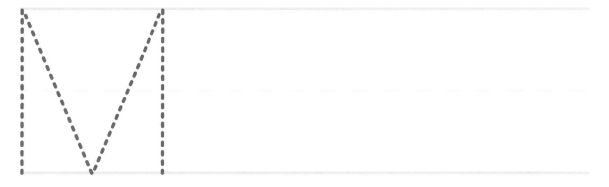

Trace, then write little letter **m**.

Draw paths to every M and m.

The Letter N

BIG

N n
littile

nightgown

Trace, then write big letter N.

Trace, then write little letter n.

Circle every N and n.

n i

f s

U J

N

I n

m j K

N

The Letter O

BIG

little

Trace, then write big letter O.

ostrich

Trace, then write little letter o.

Color every owl that has an O or o.

The Letter P

BIG

P p
little

present

Trace, then write big letter P.

P

Trace, then write little letter p.

p

Circle every **P** and **p**.

M, N, O, and P

ball
fall
tall
small

day
way
play
say

tent
sent
went

hop
top
pop

Letter Hunt!

Circle every word that has an **E** or **e**.

Now let's go on a letter hunt!
Look all around your house for things
that have words with **E** or **e**.
Look on boxes, book covers, and posters, too.

49

Q, R, and S

What's coming next?
Can you guess?
It's the letters
Q, R, and S!

Color each letter.

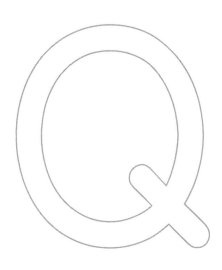

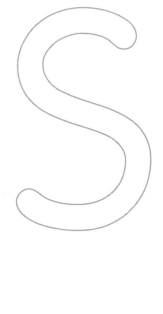

Color the letters **Q**, **R**, and **S**.

QUEEN

RABBIT

SHEEP

The Letter Q

BIG

Q

little

q

QUACK
QUACK

quack

Trace, then write big letter Q.

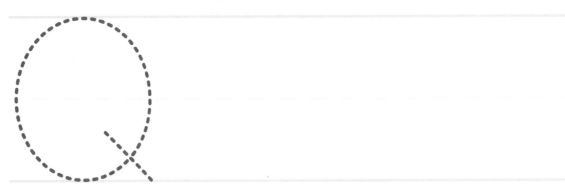

Trace, then write little letter q.

Draw paths to every Q and q.

The Letter R

BIG

R little r

rhinoceros

Trace, then write big letter **R**.

Trace, then write little letter **r**.

Connect each reindeer to an R or r.

p

r

B

V

R

Q

e

c

Y

R

r

u

The Letter S

BIG

S

little

s

squirrel

Trace, then write big letter S.

Trace, then write little letter s.

Circle every S and s.

s h
m y
b z
b s l

D
L
Q
S

Q, R, and S

YOU DID IT!

T, U, and V

When you see an umbrella, a van, or a tree, it helps to know the letters T, U, and V.

Color each letter.

Color the letters T, U, and V.

TURTLE

UMBRELLA

VIOLIN

The Letter T

BIG   little

T t

train

Trace, then write big letter T.

Trace, then write little letter t.

Color every tomato that has a T or t.

The Letter U

BIG

U

little

u

umbrella

Trace, then write big letter U.

Trace, then write little letter u.

Circle every U and u.

The Letter V

BIG

V little V

vulture

Trace, then write big letter V.

Trace, then write little letter v.

Draw paths to every V and v.

T, U, and V

YOU DID IT!

65

Hit the Road!

How many red cars do you see?
How many blue cars do you see?

Now look out your window.
How many cars are there?
How many white cars go by in two
minutes? How many black cars?

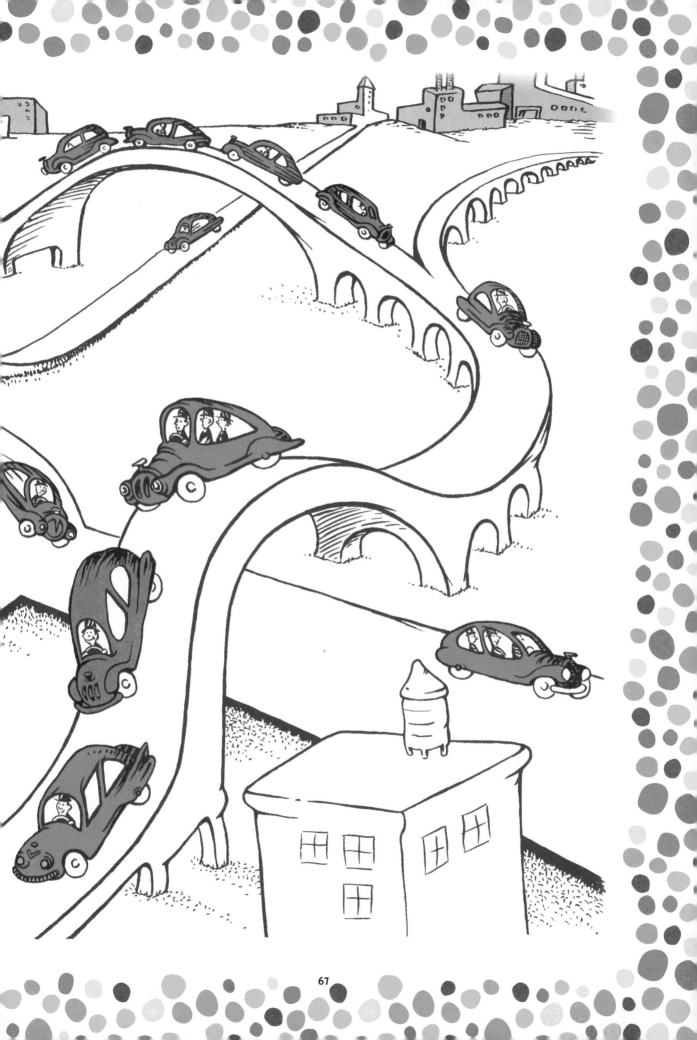

W, X, Y, and Z

To finish the alphabet, repeat after me: W, X, Y, and Z!

Color each letter.

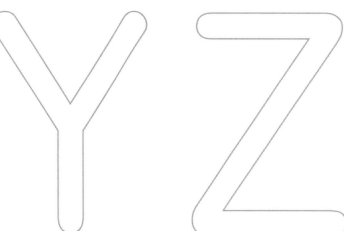

Color the letters W, X, Y, and Z.

WHALE

XYLOPHONE

YAK

ZEBRA

The Letter W

BIG
Ww
little

window

Trace, then write big letter W.

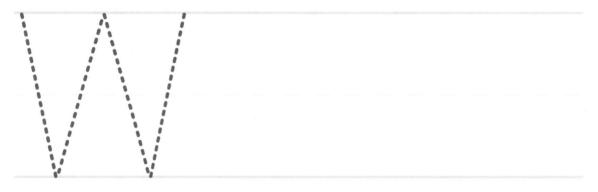

Trace, then write little letter w.

Connect each walrus to a W or w.

S

Z

D

W

g

W

p

k

W

R

W

o

The Letter X

BIG

X x little

xylophone

Trace, then write big letter X.

Trace, then write little letter x.

Circle every **X** and **x**.

a f

p x

X M

H

u K

w

x g

The Letter Y

BIG

Y  little

Y y

yell

Trace, then write big letter Y.

Trace, then write little letter y.

Color every yawning yak that has a Y or y.

y

o

t

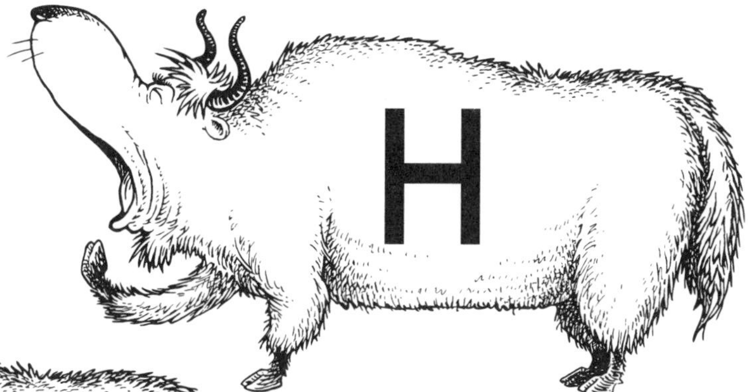

H

Y

The Letter Z

BIG

Z little

Z z

zebra

Trace, then write big letter **Z**.

Z

Trace, then write little letter **z**.

z

Circle every Z and z.

f u z Z A
a L W
z t
o Q P g z
d Z
z Y Z u
X R
r u z
Z R M

W, X, Y, and Z

YOU DID IT!

Listen to the Letters A to L

There are so many sounds for you to explore.

So listen with your ears—that's what they are for!

Point to each letter and say the sound it makes.

 A

 B

 C

 D

 E

 F

 G

 H

 I

J

K

L

The Sounds of A and B

Can you say the sound of the letter A?

apple   avocado

Draw a line from the letter **A** to the things that start with the sound of that letter.

A

Can you say the sound of the letter B?

ball   bee

Color the things that start with the sound of the letter B.

The Sounds of C and D

Can you say the sound of the letter C?

cake

camel

Color the things that start with the sound of the letter C.

Can you say the sound of the letter D?

dog   dress

Draw something special that starts with the
sound of the letter D.

The Sounds of E and F

Can you say the sound of the letter E?

 elephant

egg

Draw something special that starts with the sound of the letter E.

Can you say the sound of the letter **F**?

feathers

fish

Circle the things that start with the sound of the letter **F**.

The Sounds of G and H

Can you say the sound of the letter G?

goat   glasses

Color the things that start with the sound of the letter G.

Can you say the sound of the letter H?

hat   house

Draw a line from the letter H to the things that start with the sound of that letter.

H

The Sounds of I and J

Can you say the sound of the letter I?

ice   iguana

Draw a line from the letter I to the things that start with the sound of that letter.

I

Can you say the sound of the letter **J**?

jam

jellyfish

Draw something special that starts with the sound of the letter **J**.

The Sounds of K and L

Can you say the sound of the letter K?

kitten   key

Color the things that start with the sound of the letter K.

Can you say the sound of the letter L?

lime

lion

Circle the things that start with the sound of the letter L.

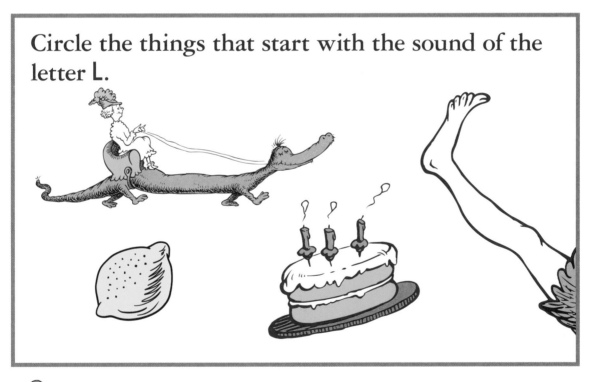

 **Listen to the Letters A to L**

YOU DID IT!

All By My Shelf!

Decorate this bookcase. Color the books, then add a flower to the vase.

Now let's make a bookcase for your very own books! Decorate a cardboard box with stickers, and draw some pictures using crayons. It's the perfect place for your favorite books.

Listen to the Letters M to Z

When you need to hear sounds that are all made by letters, you should use your two ears. (There's nothing that's better.)

Point to each letter and say the sound it makes.

M N O P

Q R S T U V W X Y Z

The Sounds of M and N

Can you say the sound of the letter M?

mitt   milk

Draw a line from the letter M to the things that start with the sound of that letter.

Can you say the sound of the letter N?

needle   net

Color the thing that starts with the sound of the letter N.

The Sounds of O and P

Can you say the sound of the letter O?

owl

ostrich

Color the thing that starts with the sound of the letter O.

Can you say the sound of the letter P?

paint   picture

Draw a line from the letter **P** to the things that start with the sound of that letter.

P

The Sounds of Q and R

Can you say the sound of the letter Q?

queen   quack

Draw something that starts with the sound of the letter Q.

Can you say the sound of the letter **R**?

rhinoceros   rabbit

Circle the things that start with the sound of the letter **R**.

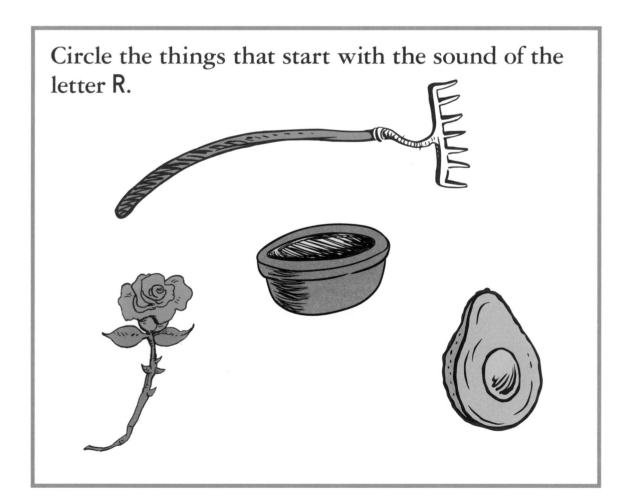

The Sounds of S and T

Can you say the sound of the letter S?

sign   sing

Color the things that start with the sound of the letter S.

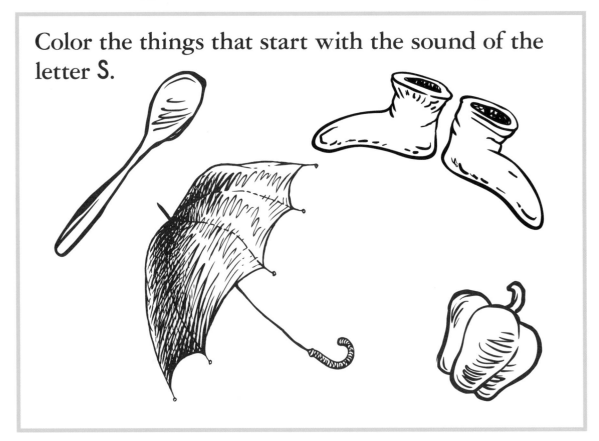

Can you say the sound of the letter T?

truck   turtle

Draw something special that starts with the sound of the letter T.

The Sounds of U and V

Can you say the sound of the letter U?

umbrella   underwear

Draw a line from the letter **U** to the things that start with the sound of that letter.

U

Can you say the sound of the letter V?

violin

vulture

Circle the thing that starts with the sound of the letter V.

The Sounds of W and X

Can you say the sound of the letter W?

whale

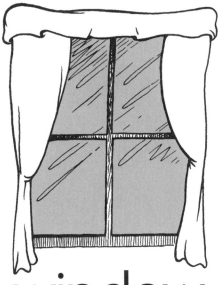

window

Circle the thing that starts with the sound of the letter W.

Can you say the sound of the letter X?

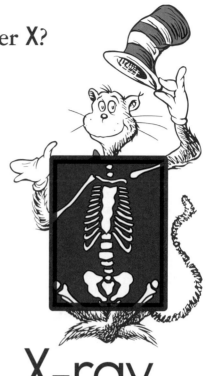

xylophone   X-ray

Color the thing that has the sound of the letter X.

The Sounds of Y and Z

Can you say the sound of the letter Y?

yam

yell

Draw a line from the letter Y to the thing that starts with the sound of that letter.

Y

Can you say the sound of the letter Z?

zipper

zucchini

Color the thing that starts with the sound of the letter **Z**.

Rhyming

Let's take the time
to play and rhyme!

Circle the two things that rhyme.

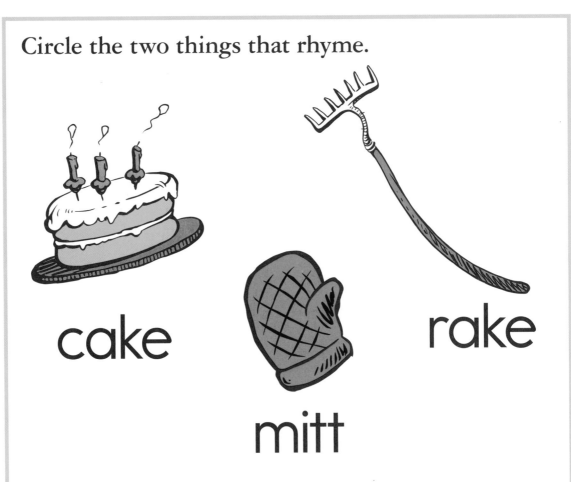

cake

mitt

rake

Draw lines to connect the things that rhyme.

grin

cup

pig

pin

pup

fig

Rhyme with "AT"

What rhymes with "hat"?

hat

Circle the things that rhyme with "hat."

bat

pan

cat

Rhyme with "IT"

What rhymes with "mitt"?

mitt

Put an X on things that rhyme with "mitt."

knit

sit

bee

Rhyme with "UP"

What rhymes with "cup"?

cup

Circle the thing that rhymes with "cup."

bowl

pup

jam

Rhyme with "ALL"

What rhymes with "ball"?

ball

Put an X on the things that rhyme with "ball."

book

small

tall

Rhyme with "IN"

What rhymes with "pin"?

pin

Circle the things that rhyme with "pin."

shoe

thin

grin

Rhyme with "OP"

What rhymes with "hop"?

hop

Put an X on the things that rhyme with "hop."

top

mop

pig

Rhyme with "ED"

What rhymes with "bed"?

bed

Circle the things that rhyme with "bed."

head

red

tail

Rhyme with "IG"

What rhymes with "pig"?

pig

Put an X on the things that rhyme with "pig."

fig

wig

ape

Rhymes

Draw lines to connect
the things that rhyme.

cat

pup

pig

hat

cup

bed

red

thin

fig

grin

 **Rhyming**

Balancing Act!

Count the clocks. Count the blocks. Count the bricks.

Now see if you can balance, too!

Get a book. Can you stand with it balanced on your head? Can you balance two books on your head? Can you balance three books on your head?

Certificate of Achievement

★

is presented to

_____

NAME

for becoming a

Remarkable Reader!

MATH

Some have **TWO** feet, and some have **FOUR**. Some have **SIX** feet, and some have **MORE**.

Numbers: 1, 2, and 3

Counting is easy, you will see. Let's start with the numbers 1, 2, and 3!

Circle the numbers 1, 2, and 3.

1 2 3 4 5

6 7 8 9 10

Color every **1** blue. Color every **2** red.
Color every **3** green.

Numbers: 1

1

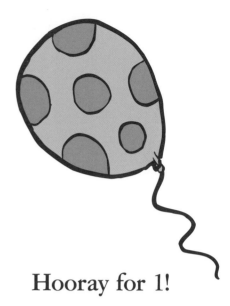

Hooray for 1!

Trace, then write the number 1.

Circle 1 lemon. Circle 1 flower.

Numbers: 2

2

Hooray for 2!

Trace, then write the number **2**.

Put an X on 2 elephants. Put an X on 2 dogs.

Numbers: 3

3

Hooray for 3!

Trace, then write the number **3**.

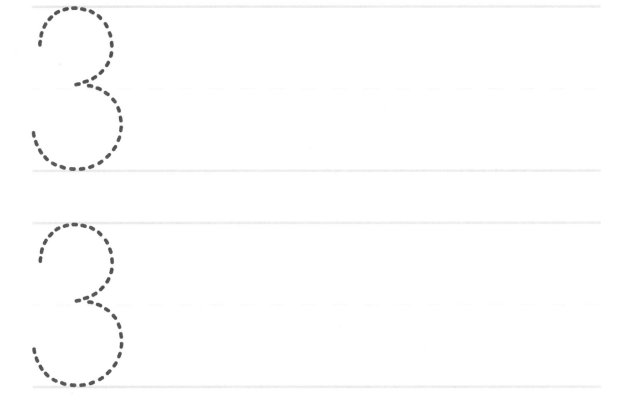

Draw a line from the number 3 to the groups of three.

Numbers: 1, 2, and 3

Honk! Tweet! Plink!

Point to each instrument, then make the sound that you think that instrument makes.

Now create your own music makers! Gather things such as pots, pans, and straws. How many different kinds of sounds can you make with them?

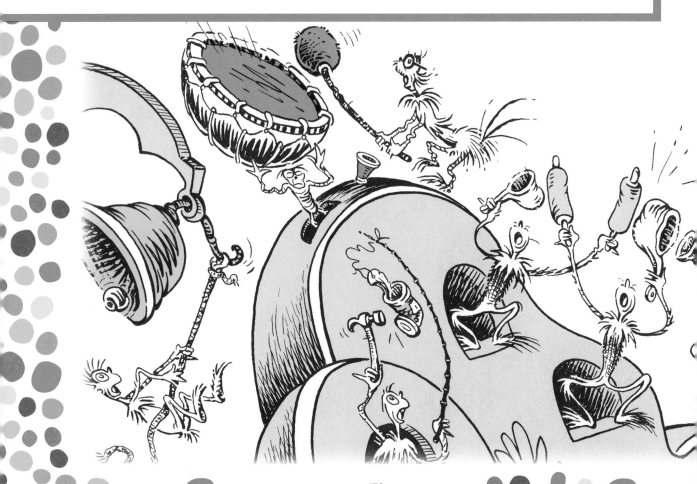

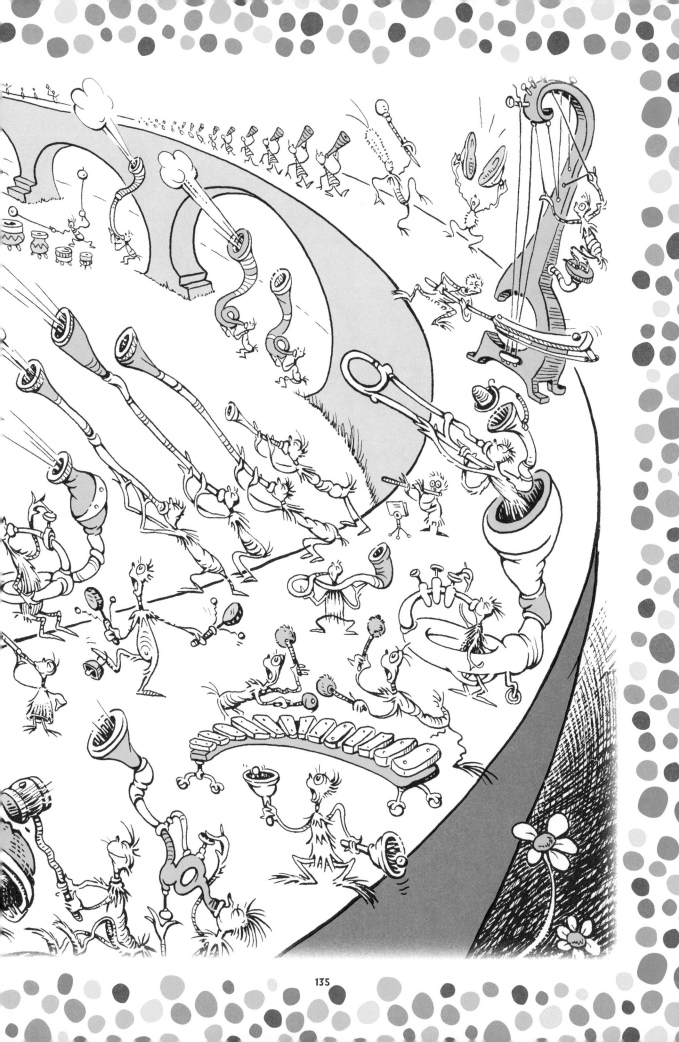

Numbers: 4, 5, and 6

> Don't be afraid. Don't make a fuss.
> Come learn **4**, **5**, and **6** with us!

Circle the numbers **4**, **5**, and **6**.

1 2 3 4 5

6 7 8 9 10

Color every 4 blue. Color every 5 red.
Color every 6 green.

5 5 4
6
5
4 4
5
6
5
6

Numbers: 4

4

Hooray for 4!

Trace, then write the number 4.

Circle 4 clocks. Circle 4 fish.

Numbers: 5

5

Hooray for 5!

Trace, then write the number **5**.

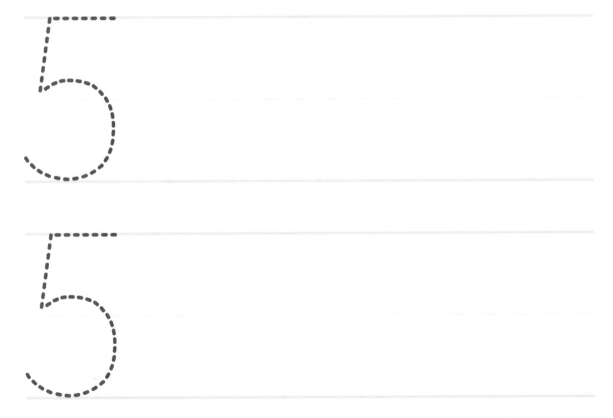

Put an X on **5** camels. Put an X on **5** bees.

Numbers: 6

Hooray for 6!

Trace, then write the number 6.

Draw a line from the number **6** to the groups of six.

Numbers: 4, 5, and 6

YOU DID IT!

Numbers: 7, 8, 9, and 10

You're doing great. You're almost done. The numbers 7, 8, 9, and 10 are lots of fun!

Circle the numbers 7, 8, 9, and 10.

1 2 3 4 5

6 7 8 9 10

Color every **7** blue. Color every **8** green.
Color every **9** red. Color every **10** yellow.

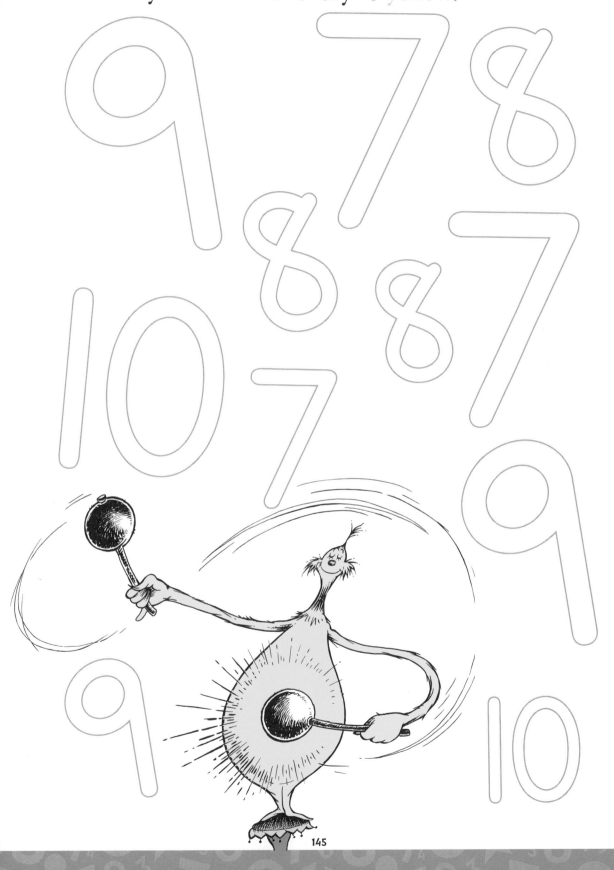

145

Numbers: 7

7

Hooray for 7!

Trace, then write the number **7**.

Circle **7** balloons. Circle **7** vases.

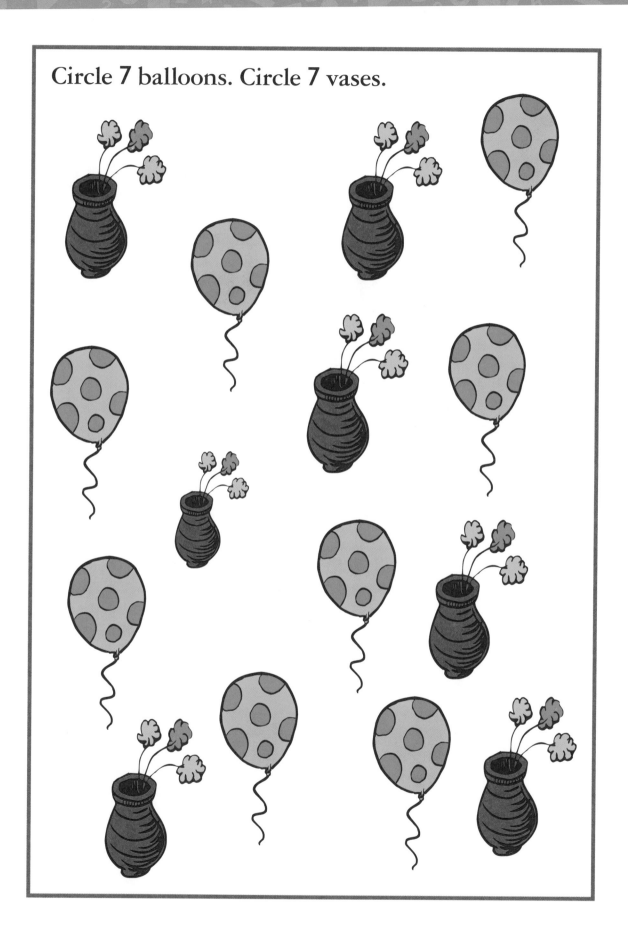

Numbers: 8

8

Hooray for 8!

Trace, then write the number **8**.

Put an X on 8 goats. Put an X on 8 cakes.

Numbers: 9

9

Hooray for 9!

Trace, then write the number **9**.

150

Draw a line from the number 9 to the groups of nine.

Numbers: 10

10

Hooray for 10!

Trace, then write the number 10.

Circle 10 umbrellas. Circle 10 mitts.

Numbers: 7, 8, 9, and 10

YOU DID IT!

Rhyme Time!

Point to the things in the picture that rhyme. How many "all" words do you see?

Now it's rhyme time. Look around your house for pairs of things that rhyme. Pie and eye? Cup and pup? Chair and hair?

How many rhymes did you discover?

Shapes: Triangle, Circle, Square, Star, Heart

All around, and in this book, are lots of shapes. Come and take a look.

Color every circle yellow.

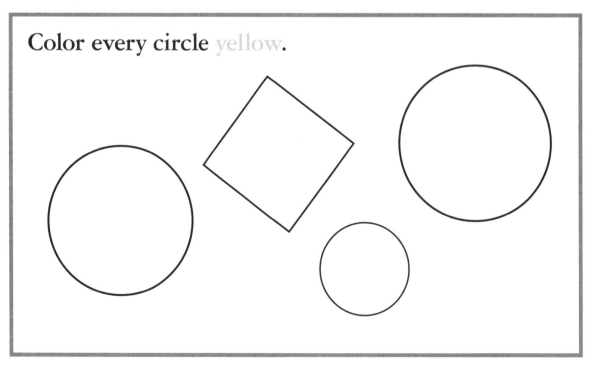

Color every square purple. Color every triangle green.
Color every star blue. Color every heart red.

Shapes: Triangle

This is a triangle.

Trace a triangle.

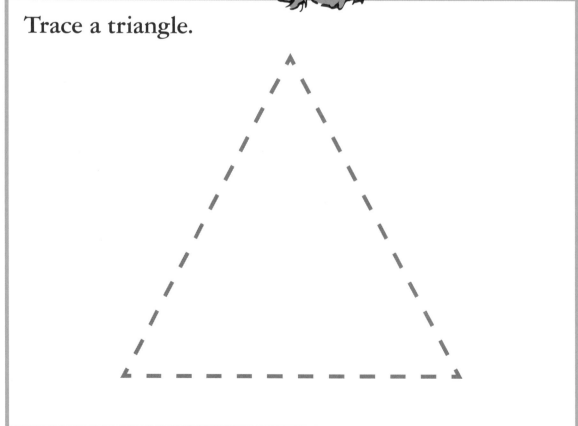

Circle how many sides a triangle has.

1   2

3   4

Put an X on all the triangles.

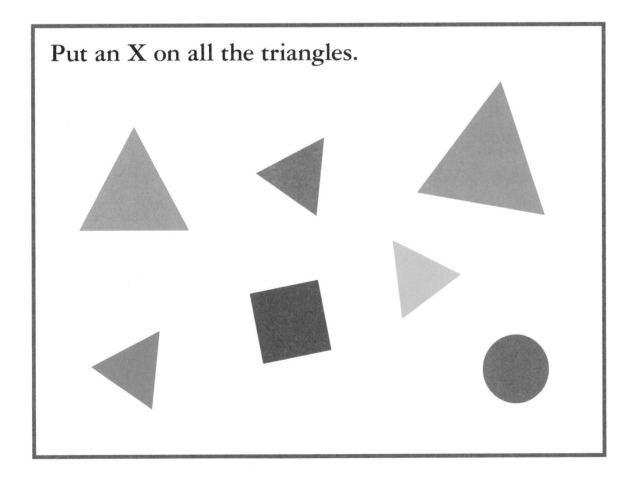

Shapes: Circle

This is a circle.

Trace a circle.

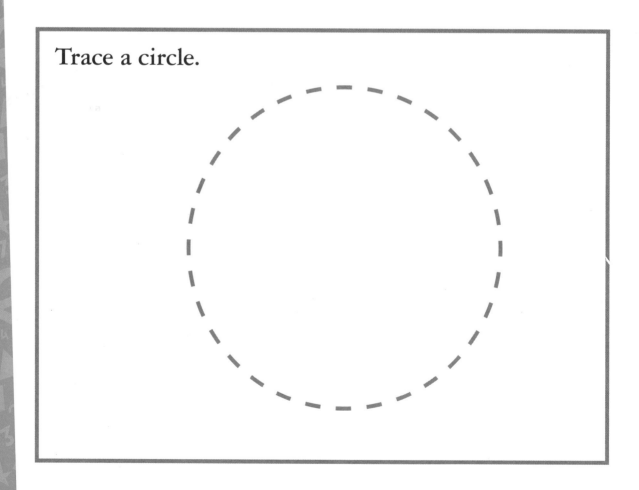

You Did It! Stickers

Place your stickers at the end of each lesson and on your certificates.

READING

MATH

FEELINGS

SCIENCE

Put an X on all the things that are in the shape of a circle.

Shapes: Square

This is a square.

Trace a square.

Circle how many sides a square has.

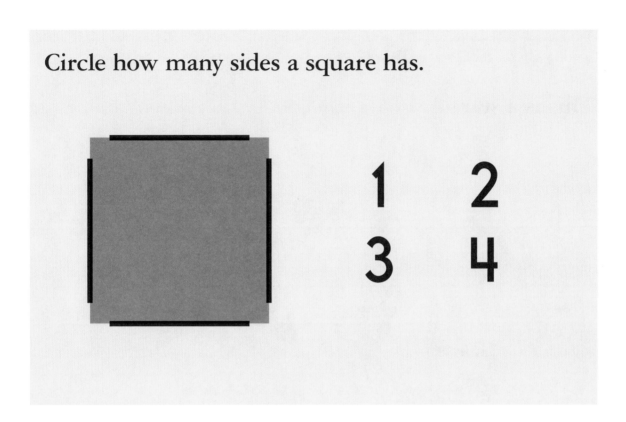

1   2

3   4

Put an X on all the squares.

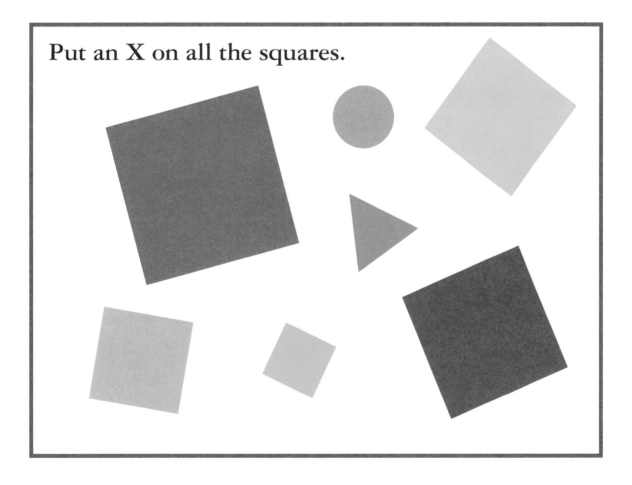

Shapes: Star

This is a star.

Trace a star.

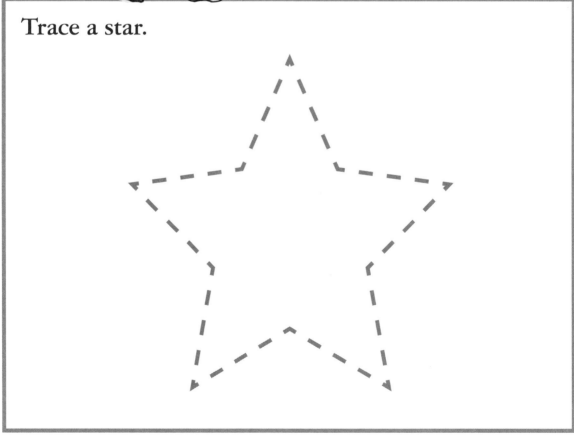

Circle all the things that are in the
shape of a star.

Shapes: Heart

This is a heart.

Trace a heart.

Put an X on all the hearts.

Shapes: Triangle, Circle, Square, Star, Heart

YOU DID IT!

Shapes: Diamond, Rectangle, Pentagon, Hexagon, Oval

Shapes are everywhere. Yes, it's true.
Rectangles, ovals, and diamonds, too!

Color every rectangle blue.

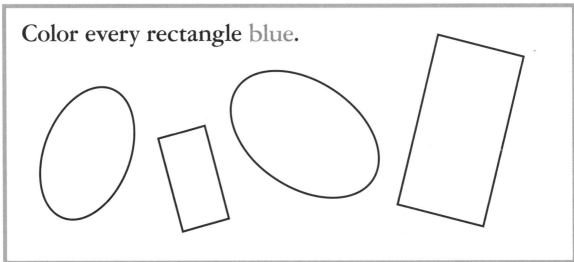

Color every diamond purple. Color every oval green.
Color every pentagon yellow. Color every hexagon red.

Shapes: Diamond

This is a diamond.

Trace a diamond.

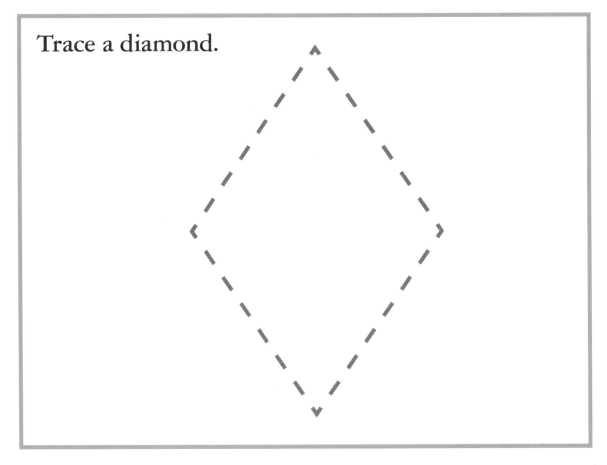

Circle how many sides a diamond has.

1   2

3   4

5   6

Put an X on all the diamonds.

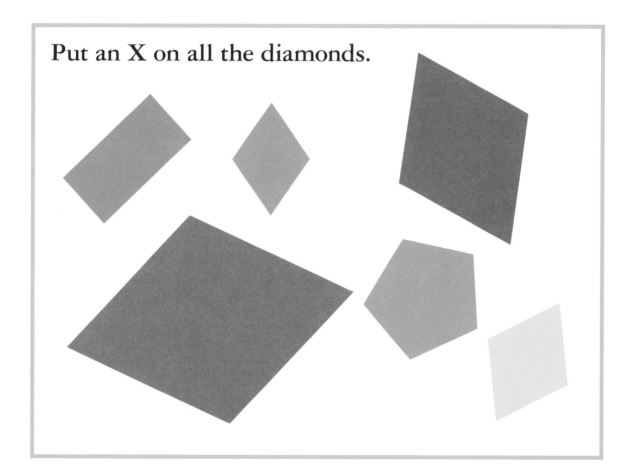

Shapes: Rectangle

These are rectangles.

Trace a rectangle.

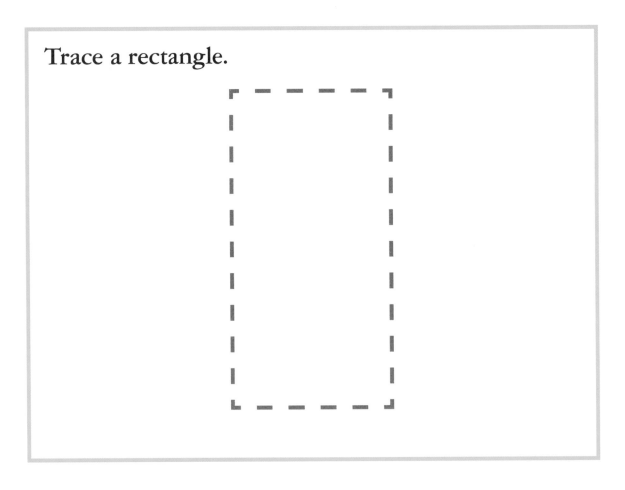

Circle how many sides a rectangle has.

1   2

3   4

5   6

Put an X on all the rectangles.

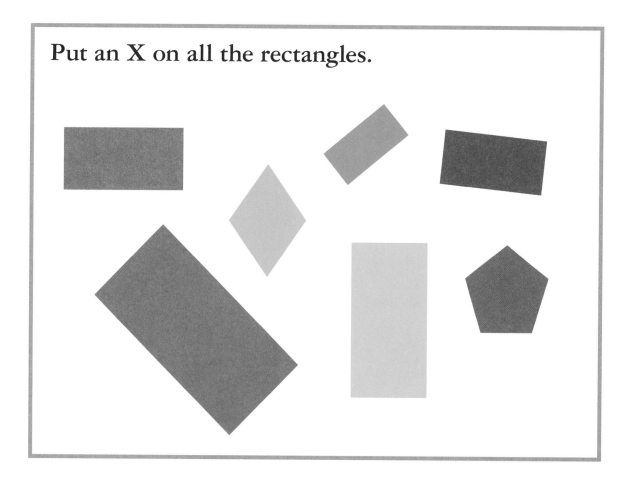

Shapes: Pentagon

This is a pentagon.

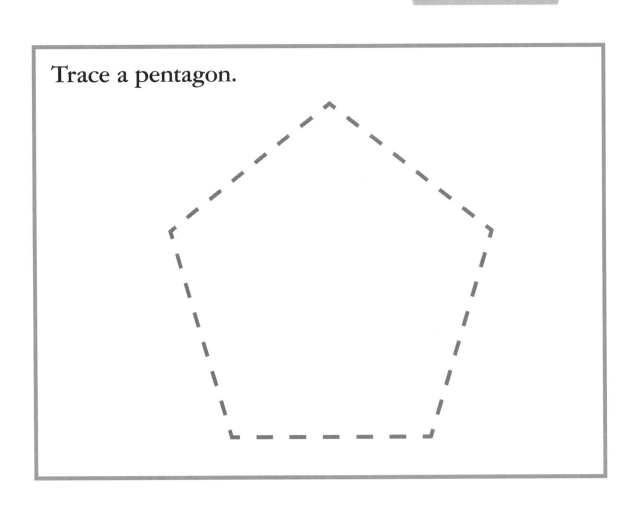

Trace a pentagon.

Circle how many sides a pentagon has.

1   2

3   4

5   6

Put an X on all the pentagons.

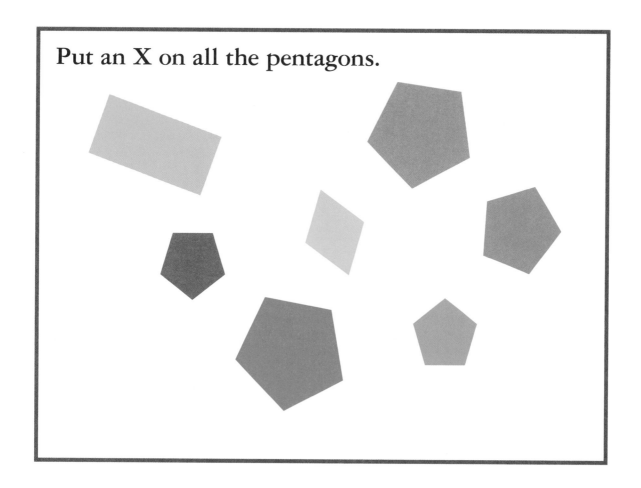

Shapes: Hexagon

This is a hexagon.

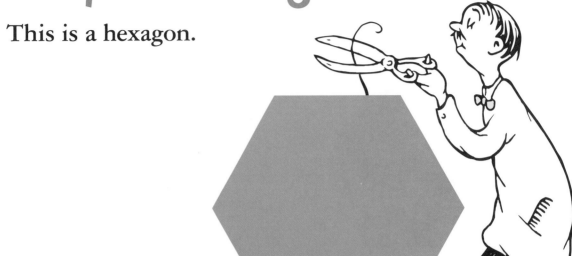

Trace a hexagon.

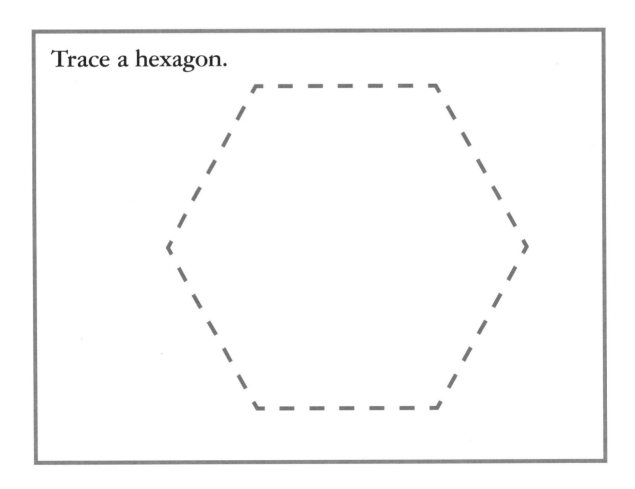

Circle how many sides a hexagon has.

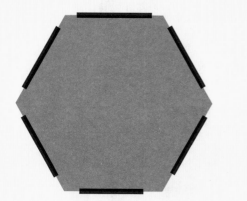

1   2

3   4

5   6

Put an X on all the hexagons.

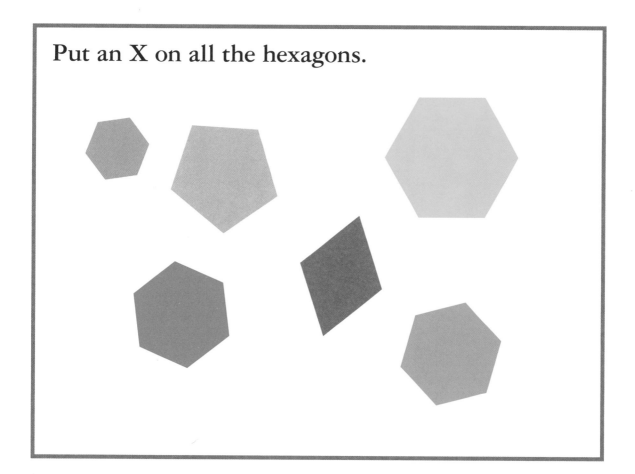

Shapes: Oval

These are ovals.

Trace an oval.

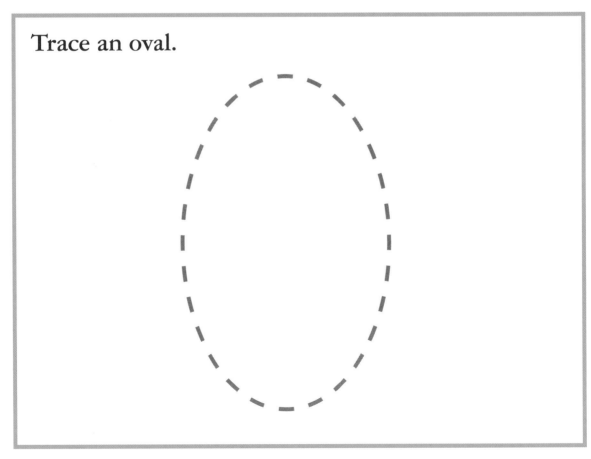

Put an X on all the things that are in the shape of an oval.

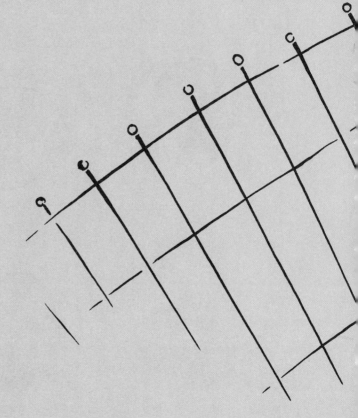

Teeth Tracker!

How many teeth does this big beast have?

Now let's learn about you!
Look in a mirror. Count YOUR teeth.

How many are on the top?
How many are on the bottom?
Do you have more teeth than toes?

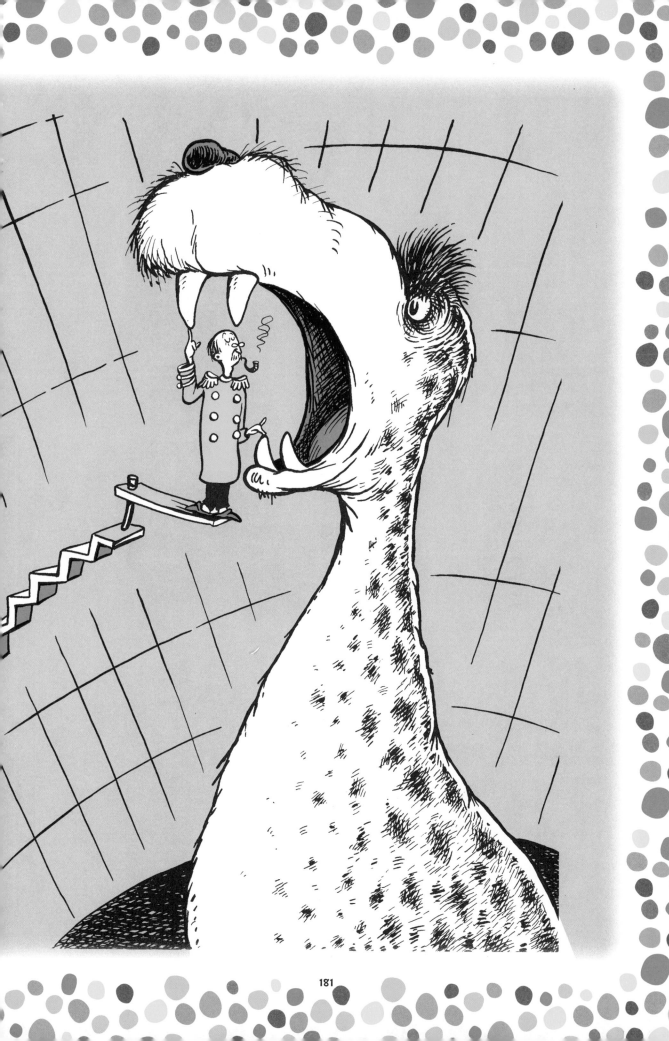

Certificate of Achievement ⭐

is presented to

_____

NAME

for becoming a

Math
Magician!

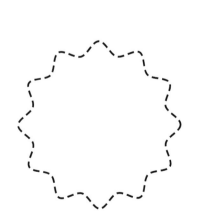

FEELINGS

Today you are YOU, that is TRUER than true. There is NO ONE alive who is YOU-ER than YOU.

Collect your stickers at the end of each lesson.

Happy, Sad, Mad

What makes you happy?

What makes you sad?

What are some things that make you mad?

Color every happy face.

Circle every face that looks sad or mad.

Happy

Some things make
us happy.

Circle all the things that make you happy.

Put an X on all the things that make you unhappy.

Sad

Some things
make us sad.

Circle the face that looks sad.

Draw what's making this creature sad.

Mad

Some things
make us mad.

Put an X on every face that looks mad.

Draw what's making this creature mad.

Make Friends

This fish is giving someone a ride. Draw who it is.

Draw what's inside this huge bottle.

Make Plans

Finish this track to reach the other side.

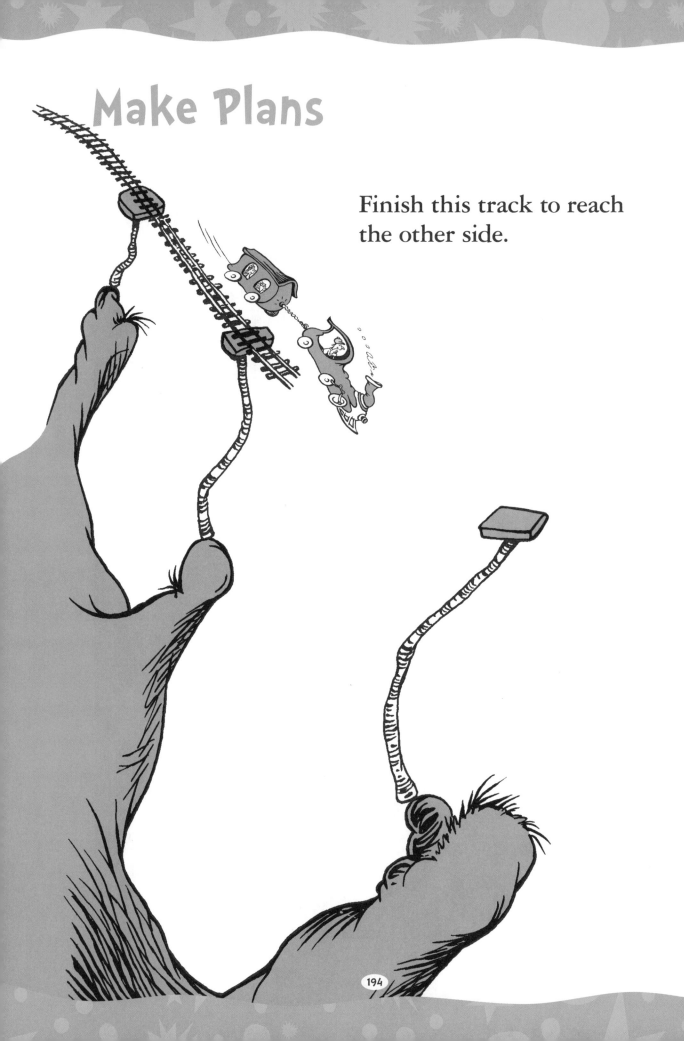

Draw what's waiting at the end.

Make Noise

Draw the sounds that come from
each of these crazy instruments.

Draw what this creature is yelling about.

Happy, Sad, Mad

Sleepy, Scared, Surprised

When you get tired, do you hop in bed?

Do worried thoughts fill up your head?

Color every sleepy face.

Circle every face that looks scared.

Sleepy

Sometimes
we feel sleepy.

Circle everyone who looks sleepy.

Draw who is sleeping in these beds.

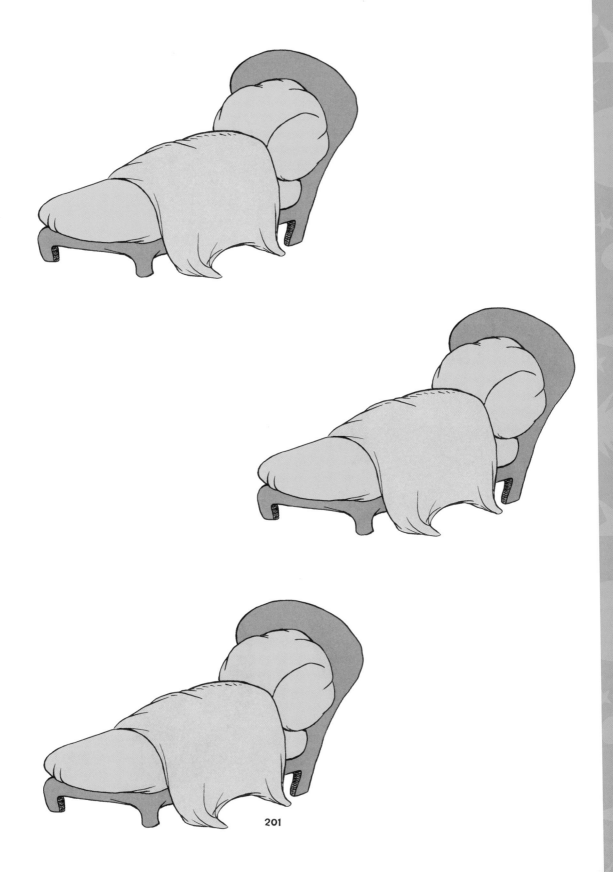

Scared

Sometimes
we feel scared.

Put an X on
every face that
looks scared.

Draw what's making this creature scared.

Surprised

Sometimes
we feel surprised.

Put an X on every face that looks surprised.

Draw why this person is surprised.

Make a Map

Trace the trail for the bike to reach the finish line.

Make a Mistake

Oops! Draw a line between things that went wrong.

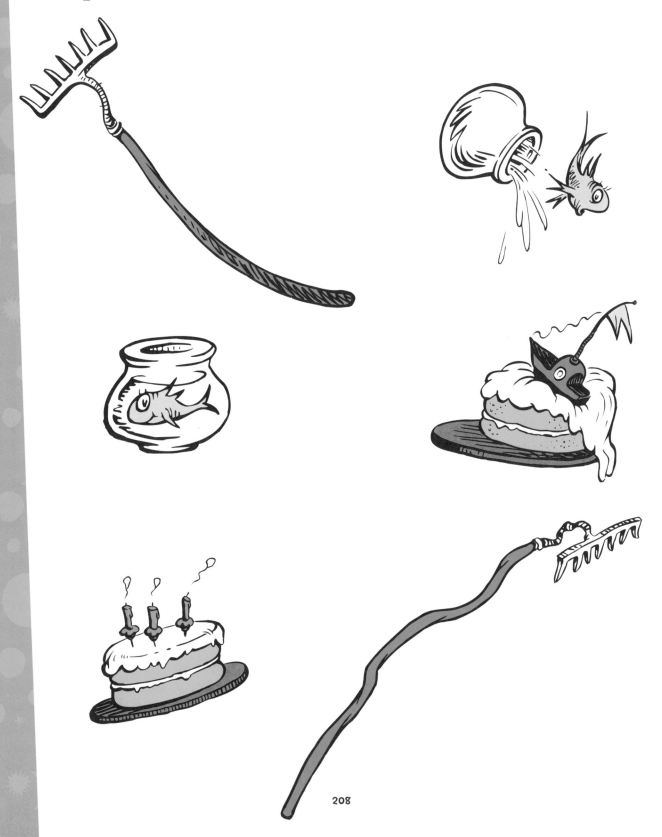

Sleepy, Scared, Surprised

YOU DID IT!

209

Tale of a Tail!

Using your finger, trace this strange creature's tail, from its beginning to its end.

Now draw your own animals.
Give one a short tail. Give one a long tail.
Give one a very, very lo-o-o-o-ng tail!

Excited, Busy, Proud

When you're excited or busy or proud, do you ever want to shout out loud?

Color every excited face.

Circle every turtle that looks proud.

Excited

Sometimes
we are excited.

Circle everyone who looks excited.

Put an X on everything that makes you excited.

Busy

Sometimes
we are busy.

Put an X on everyone who looks busy.

Circle all the people in this busy place.

217

Proud

Sometimes
we are proud.

Circle the faces that look proud.

Draw why this creature is proud.

Get in Line

This crowd of people are excited about something.
Draw what they are excited to see.

Show Off!

What do you do best?
Draw yourself doing something as people cheer.

Draw something that will get these bored people's attention.

Join the Parade

Draw some people, animals, and floats that are in this fun parade.

Excited, Busy, Proud

YOU DID IT!

Laughing, Crying, Cheering

What things can make you laugh or cry, or cheer for people passing by?

Color every laughing face.

Circle everyone who looks like they are crying.

Laughing

Some things
make us laugh.

Circle everyone who is laughing.

Put an X on all the things that make you laugh.

Crying

Some things
make us cry.

Circle the one who is crying.

Draw what's making this creature cry.

Cheering

Some things make
us cheer.

Put an X on everyone who is cheering.

Draw why these creatures are cheering.

Pull!

All these wheeled contraptions are carrying something very heavy. Draw what it is.

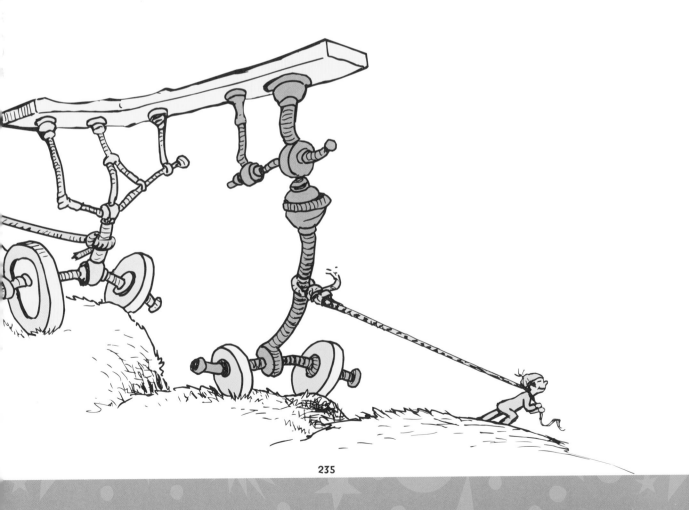

Hang in There!

Draw things that are bothering this creature.

Draw what this person is tied to.

Yum!

Draw what's being served.

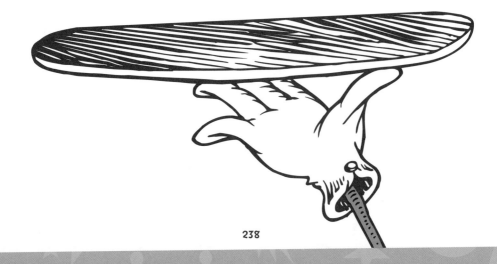

Put an X on all the things that look yummy.

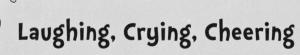

Laughing, Crying, Cheering

Yes, We Can!

How many cans are on the shelves?

Now it's time to try it where you live.

Go to your kitchen and count the cans.
Do you have more cans than boxes?
Do you have more boxes than bottles?

Certificate of Achievement ★

is presented to

NAME

for becoming a

Fantastic Friend!

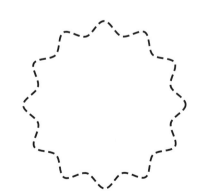

Think and **WONDER**. Wonder and **THINK**. How much **WATER** can fifty-five elephants **DRINK**?

Collect your stickers at the end of each lesson.

Every Body

Hooray for your body, from your head to your toes and from the tips of your fingers to the end of your nose.

Circle which of these things go on feet.

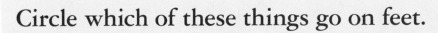

Draw a line from the clothes to the body part they belong on.

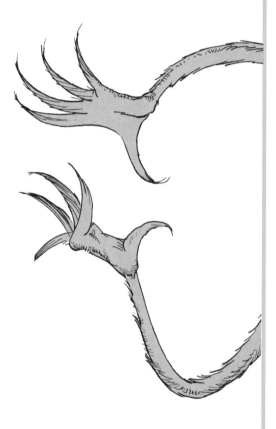

Eyes and Hair

Circle all the eyes.

Draw hair on these heads.

Mouths and Noses

Circle all the noses.

Draw different mouths on these faces.

Hands

Circle all the hands.

Wings and Tails

Color all the animals that have wings.

Circle all the tails on these animals.

Feet

Circle all the feet.

Every Body

Living Things

From under the ocean to up in a tree, there are wonderful creatures. Explore them with me!

Circle all the things that can move about.

Match the silhouette to the creature.

Moving Around

Circle all the creatures that are flying.

Circle all the creatures that are swimming.

Circle all the creatures that are walking.

Where Things Live

Draw some things that live in this water.

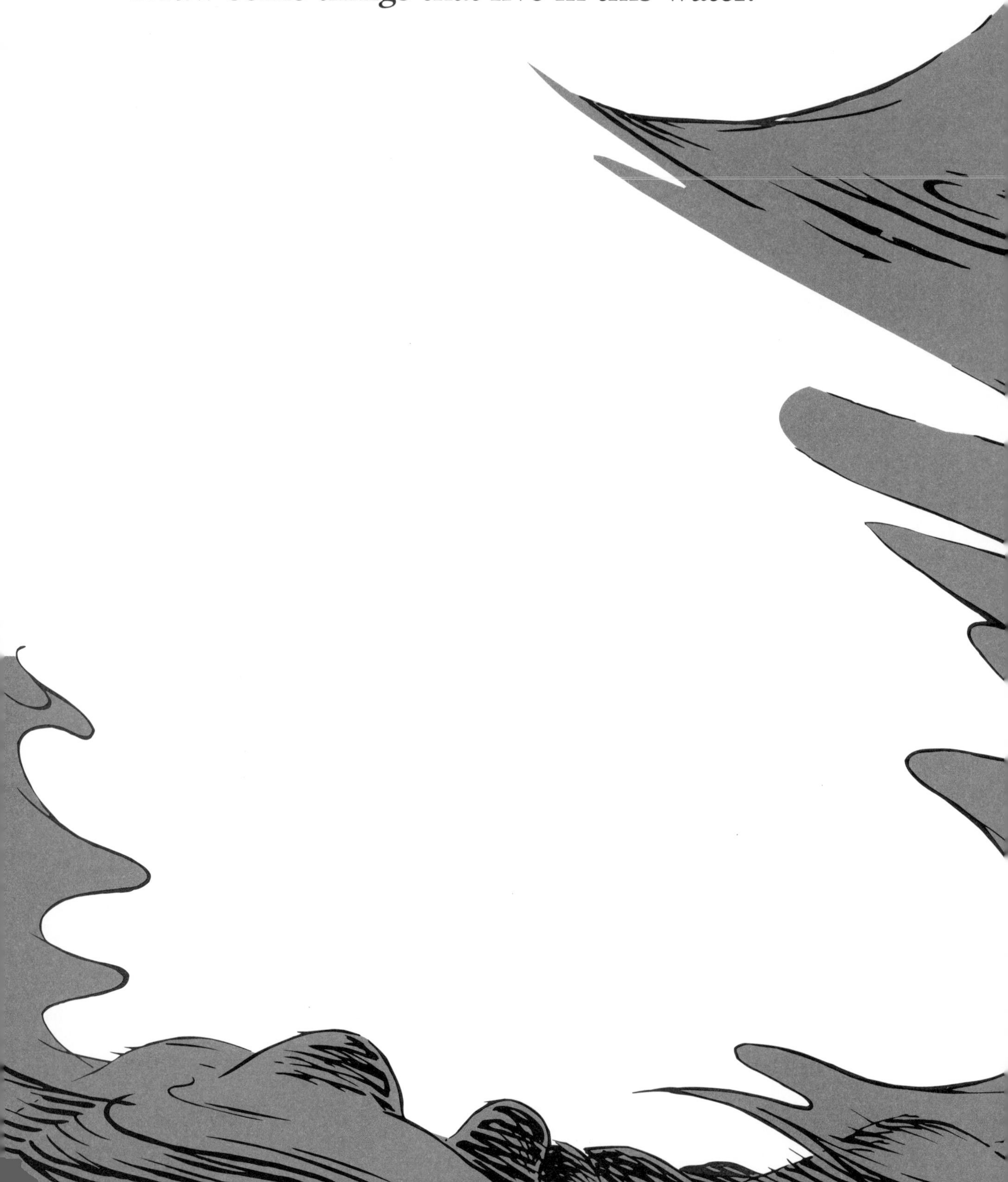

Draw some things that live in this tree.

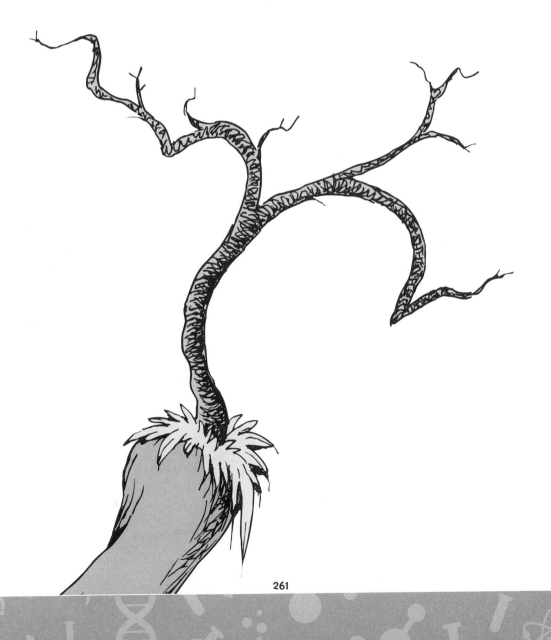

Home, Sweet Home

Draw lines from each of these animals to where you think they like to hang out.

What Things Eat

Draw something for everyone to eat.

Making Tracks

Circle the correct animals that make these tracks.

Sounds

Draw a line from each sound to what made it.

 **Hoo Hoo Hoo**

 **Choo Choo**

 **Buzz Buzz**

 **Oink Oink**

Living Things

YOU DID IT!

Hello, X and O!

How many Xs and Os can you find here?
Look carefully. Some are big, but some are tiny.

Now let's play an X-and-O game.

Find a book in your house.
Flip through the pages, and see if you can spot
three Xs and three Os.

Describing Things

The world is exciting and full of surprises, with patterns and shapes and all colors and sizes.

Circle the animal that has spots.

Circle every animal that has stripes.

Fast and Slow

Color the things that are fast.

Color the things that are slow.

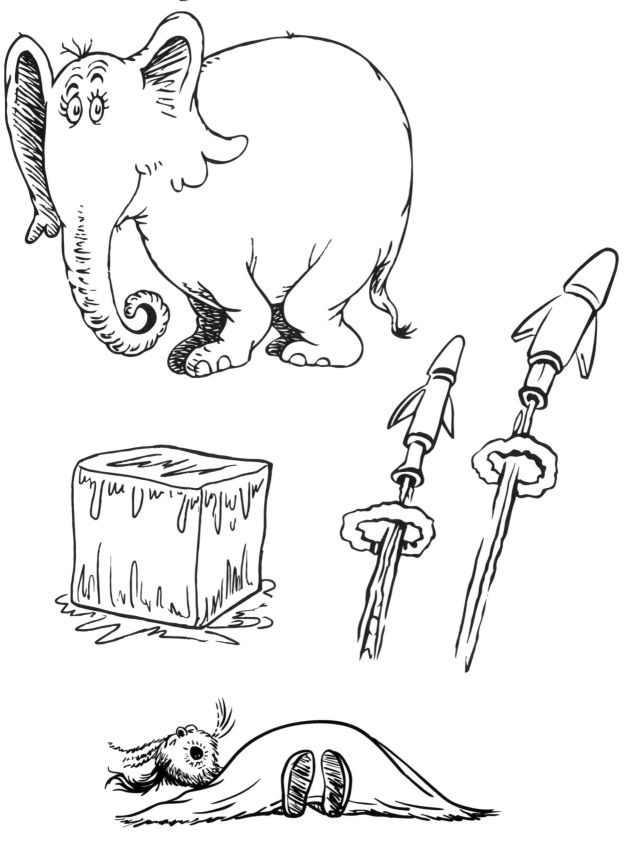

Hot and Cold

Put an X on the
things that are hot.

Circle the things that are cold.

Shhhh!

Put an X on all the things that are loud.

279

Tall and Short

Draw someone taller than this man.

Circle the tallest creature green.
Circle the shortest creature blue.

Draw someone shorter than this woman.

Straight and Curvy

Put an X on the path that is straight.
Circle the road that is curved.

Circle all the paintings with straight lines.

Describing Things

Tools and Machines

Building new things is a whole lot of fun. Hooray for the tools that get the job done.

Circle all the tools you have in your home.

YOU NEED ATHNEED

Tools

Draw a line from each tool to what it can be used for.

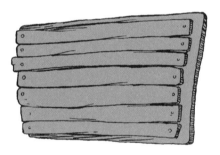

Circle all the tools.

Reach and Dig

Circle the tool that will help to pick the apples.

Circle the tool that will help to dig up the diamond.

Machines

Draw something that these machines can do.

290

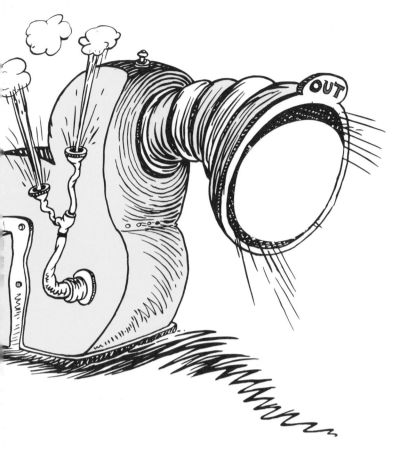

Transportation

Draw a line from each vehicle to where it can help you go.

Hop on Board

Draw a passenger for each type of transportation.

Buildings

Add buildings to make a big city.

Wheels and Wings

Circle all the vehicles that have wheels.

Put an X on all the vehicles that have wings

YOU NEED A THNEED

298

YOU
NEED
ATHNEED

Trails

Draw a line from each box to
the one that made these tracks.

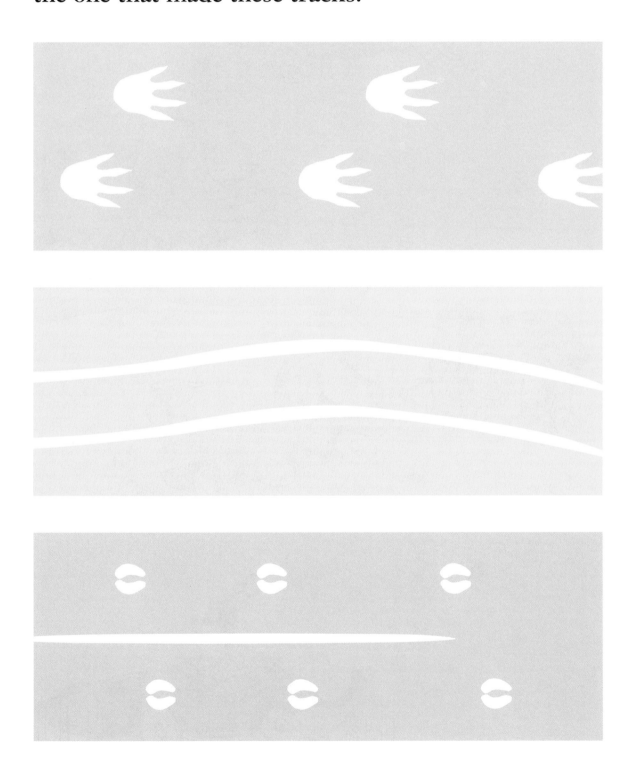

Tools and Machines

One, Two, Three—Sit!

How many chairs are going around in this circle?

Now it's time to play a game.

Put many chairs in a circle. (Pick an odd number.) Sit to start. Get up and count three chairs. Sit there. Do it again. And again. Keep going until you have sat on every chair.

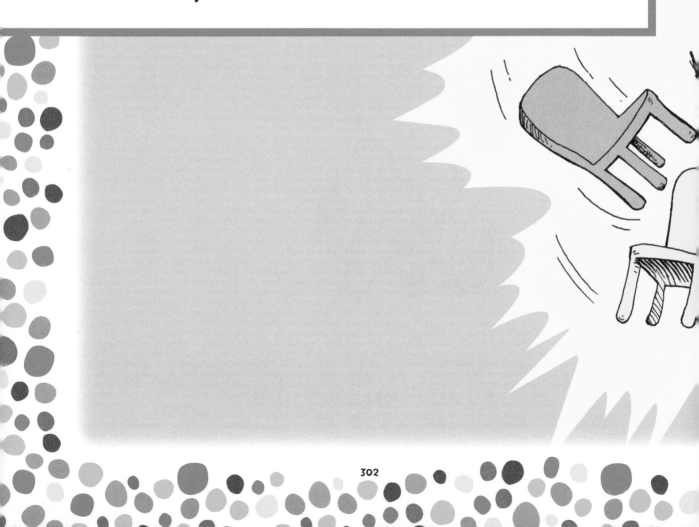

Certificate of Achievement

⭐ ⭐

is presented to

_____
NAME

for becoming a

Science Superstar!